the art of motherhood

the art of motherhood

SUSANNAH MARRIOTT

MQP

Published by **MQ Publications Limited**
12 The Ivories,
6–8 Northampton Street,
London N1 2HY
Tel: 44 (0) 20 7359 2244
Fax: 44 (0) 20 7359 1616
email: mail@mqpublications.com
website: www.mqpublications.com

Design by **Balley Design Associates**

ISBN: 1 84072 839 6

1 3 5 7 9 0 8 6 4 2

For my Mum

*Special thanks to all the Hackney mums at Happitime
Playgroup and Rushmore School, especially Stella
Olasanoye-Akintewe, Farzana Patel, Martine Gallie, Stacey
Foster, and Joy Awiah. Thanks also to Jo Leevers, Georgia
Sawyers, Mary Mathieson, Sue Clarke. Most of all, thanks
to Olive, Stella, and Berry for teaching me how to be a
mum, and to Parker for giving me time to write it down.*

Printed and bound in China

Contents

Introduction

The art of motherhood should come perfectly naturally, you'd think; an instinctive reaction to childbirth. Yet I don't know a new mother who has not sobbed at the terrifying otherness of this new state. Motherhood has been the most frustrating, bewildering, and exhausting experience of my life. But the fact that I made the journey willingly three times is testimony to the fact that it's also been the most liberating, exhilarating, and joyous undertaking—the best thing I ever did.

Stuck at home with a new baby who is crying, refusing to sleep, or feeding nonstop, which mother hasn't screamed, "Help! What should I do?" This book aims to come to the rescue with tried and tested tips that worked with my three baby girls, some passed on from my mother and her Cornish grannies before her. When I asked other mothers for their family traditions, most replied, "That was for my grandmother's generation." Only women I know from African and Asian families seem to have retained such vital knowledge. So this book is for mothers who lack a well of passed-on experience. There are ideas for massage and yoga, gentle herbs, aromatherapy, and other natural solutions from around the world that will soothe a baby to sleep, ease fractious crying, and tempt tiny palates. There are also mind-restoring meditations, pampering spa treatments, and reassuring advice from real moms to salve the effects of sleepless nights, help you cope with the chaos, and gain some space for yourself as you adjust to your new life.

ABOVE ALL, YOU NEED TIME AND SPACE
WITH YOUR BABY TO BE ABLE TO TUNE
INTO EACH OTHER.

Martine, *mother of Elsie, 6, and Rose, 2.*

1

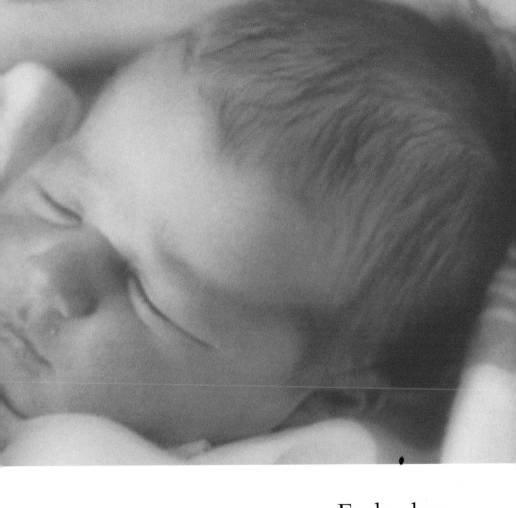

Early days

Shock of the new

Life turns upside down when you have a baby. Childbirth—the most tumultuous physical and emotional event a woman can experience—is just the beginning of immense changes that force you to take a backseat in life: from now on, you will always think of someone else before yourself. Simultaneously, that person puts you center stage: you are the very essence of someone else's existence. In the past in the West, and still throughout Asia and Africa, childbirth marks the start of a ten-day to two-month "lying-in" period of adjustment. The new mother retreats to bed to rest, recuperate, feed, and get to know her baby while the women around her cook nourishing soups to replace lost fluids and nutrients, do the heavy housework such as cleaning and washing, and even change the baby's diaper. They also offer massage, hot baths, and other pampering bodycare treatments to nurture, cherish, and rebalance the mother, making her feel special as she eases into her new role. How come we lost out? Here are some ideas that draw on those traditions to get you through the first otherworldly days and nights.

I GO HOME TO MY MOTHER FOR FORTY DAYS AFTER EACH BIRTH; SHE WON'T LET ME LIFT A FINGER.

Farzana, *mother of Hassaanah, 4, Safiyyah, 3, Abdullah, 2, and Khadeejah, 2 weeks.*

Indulge and enjoy

You've just given birth. This ranks among the most momentous days of your life, so savor every minute, even the painful parts. Doze with your sleepy baby, eat whatever takes your fancy (a box of cornflakes, three bottles of Perrier, champagne, and chocolate for me). Stare and stare with amazement and relief at this tiny thing you know so intimately and yet have never seen; scrutinize that miraculous face before it becomes familiar, wallowing in the intense eye contact that newborns give. Fill the room with flowers; demand expensive moisturizer and eye-repair creams to combat dark circles; watch TV, read *Vogue*, take long, hot baths. Don't do anything you should do—like cook, clean up, call relatives you feel obliged to speak to, answer the door, or move from bed. Don't worry if your baby doesn't wake or feed for a few hours; don't even think about bathing it (far too scary), and above all, don't feel guilty. Soon people will start ignoring you as the focus switches to the baby (you are now a mom, after all), so milk this brief "babymoon" euphoria for all it's worth (in some cultures it indeed lasts for the cycle of one moon).

I refused to get out of bed for a fortnight and they were the best weeks of my life.

Bettina, *mother of Sigrid, 4 months.*

Rest and recuperate

In societies where new mothers get support and aren't expected to carry on as normal, postnatal illness is rare. In Britain, where mothers discharged from hospital forty-eight hours after giving birth are expected to resume the role of superwoman in the kitchen, bedroom, and boardroom, one in five experiences postnatal depression. Be easy on yourself.

Caution: *if tearfulness becomes all-pervading sadness or guilt, visit a medical practitioner.*

- **Seek respite care:** in parts of India and Central America, mother and child have no contact but the midwife for ten days. Have a relative or friend move in to cook, clean, and coddle.

- **Go home:** Japanese women return to their parents for the first month.

- **Take to bed:** Chinese women take two weeks' bedrest, Hopi Indians a full month. In Italy mothers out with babies under three weeks old are frowned upon.

- **Discourage visitors:** why does everyone choose to visit on day three when the adrenaline that masked exhaustion and aches runs out, the baby wakes from newborn slumber, milk comes into rockhard breasts, no clothes fit, and you can't stop sobbing?

- **Ask good friends to deliver meals then leave:** in Eastern Europe, neighbors bring birth baskets piled with pastries. Our local church delivers homecooked meals daily for two weeks.

In Ghanaian tradition you go back to your mother's home. I retreated there five days a week and let her do everything while I slept.

Joy, *mother of Jan, 5, and Saskia, 3.*

Massage for new mothers

From Turkey to Malaysia, a mother is massaged by a close female relative for the forty-day period after childbirth. Instead of baby gifts, urge friends to book a masseur to come to your home while they mind the baby. Or ask a friend to perform a brief massage after your six-week check, using this recipe. Dilute 2 tbsp sweet almond oil with 3 drops each essential oils of frankincense, lavender, and neroli (good for rebalancing after birth). When you lack sleep, silence, or time on your own, massage is heavenly. Lie on your back and ask your friend to follow these instructions.

1 Sit behind the head, warm a little oil between your palms, and place them side by side just below the collarbones. Draw outward, circle the tops of the arms, pull in under the back of the shoulders, and draw up the back of the neck, lifting the head slightly. Release at the hairline, gliding down the neck to repeat six times.

2 Place your hands on either side of the head, then roll it slowly from one hand to the other. With the head resting on the right hand, stroke down the left side of the neck to the shoulder with the left palm. Glide back to repeat. Repeat on the other side.

3 Finally, sit by the abdomen, apply a little oil, and place your palms one above the other below the navel, fingers pointing away. Gently circle the abdomen clockwise with flat palms, lifting one hand over the other as they meet.

Javanese bath ritual

Indonesia is famed for its postbirth bodywrap treatments which, combined with daily massage, claim to tighten "baggy" skin. Try this version after your six-week check. Cajuput oil promotes sweating to remove toxins, is pain-relieving, and imitates the hormone estrogen. Peppermint oil encourages perspiration and relaxes, anesthetizing the abdominal muscles slightly. Eucalyptus oil benefits the genitourinary system, and helps repair skin tissue. These oils are strong, so do a patch test beforehand (dab a little blended oil on skin and wait twenty-four hours to see whether there is a bad reaction).

Caution: *omit eucalyptus oil with high blood pressure or epilepsy, and peppermint oil if nursing.*

INGREDIENTS

1 tbsp sweet almond oil
1 tbsp olive oil
1 tsp wheatgerm oil
3 drops each essential oils of cajuput, peppermint, and eucalyptus

juice of 1 lemon
1 tbsp baby rice
1in (2.5cm) fresh ginger root, finely grated
6yd (2m) muslin

1 Blend the oils, juice, baby rice, and ginger to make a thin paste. Massage into abdomen and lower back, from hips to navel. Let dry for 10 minutes. Bind with the cloth, starting at the hips and winding toward the ribcage.

2 Lie down for 20 minutes, and sip water. Untie the fabric (place a strainer over the plughole), shower, then massage with body lotion, using soft sculpting movements from hipbones to navel.

Coping during the night

Fired up on adrenaline all day while the baby sleeps, you collapse exhausted into bed. The moment you drift off, the baby wakes for a feed. Every hour. When you deserve the sleep of your life, you have to forfeit it for your child. Welcome to motherhood. While practiced breastfeeding mothers doze through night feeds nursing lying down, first-timers can find this impossible. Here are other ways to cope.

● **Stay warm in bed:** don't think of moving. When you are warm and relaxed, a baby drifts back to sleep more readily.

● **Support back, arm, and baby:** use mountains of pillows, bolsters, and cushions to make yourself comfortable.

● **Swaddle the baby:** lie him on a cotton crib sheet and wrap one end, then the other, across his body.

● **Keep a hot-water bottle in bed:** pop it in the crib while you feed so it's warm when you put him back.

● **Switch on a nightlight:** helps good latching on. If bottle-feeding, keep a bottle-warmer by the bed.

● **Clip a light to an engrossing book or watch TV:** I watched my favorite soap through long feeds (perhaps explaining why that daughter never settled).

● **Make a flask of hot chocolate:** he gets a comforting drink, and so do you.

● **Keep within reach:** wipes, diapers, diaper cream, babygros. But don't change the baby unless absolutely necessary.

Soothing afterpains

Some of the positions and breathing techniques helpful for birth may bring relief from the afterpains that accompany breastfeeding, as they stimulate the womb to contract to its prepregnancy size. Try the exercise below as well, to help realign the postnatal spine and counter backache. (Chinese doctors advise a month's bedrest to do the same job.)

● **Hip circles:** lying on your back, bring knees to chest, hands on shins. Slowly circle the legs clockwise, easing around the 360°. Repeat in the other direction.

● **Breathing:** focusing on the out-breath, imagine exhaling the pain, groaning if it helps. Feel your abdominal muscles pulling toward your lower back. When you can exhale no further, let the in-breath come easily. Then focus on letting everything go again with the out-breath.

● **Warmth:** in Nigeria, a cloth is soaked in boiling water, wrung dry, then used to massage the abdomen.

Realigning the spine

1 Lie on the floor, legs hip-width apart, knees bent, feet flat. Inhaling, imagine breathing into your pelvis. Exhaling, let the bones relax toward the floor and the small of your back drop. Repeat.

2 Focus on your shoulderblades, feeling the upper back widen and soften as air fills your lungs. On the exhalation, let everything melt into the floor. Repeat.

3 Exhaling, slide your shoulders toward your hips, backs of arms resting comfortably down. Tuck in your chin to lengthen the back of the neck.

Massage for new babies

Handling a new baby is terrifying; massage offers one of the best ways to get to know an infant, and across Asia and Africa is practiced daily from birth. Massage permits prolonged eye contact, gives confidence in handling tiny limbs, and enables you to demonstrate love in a practical way when you feel numb and unsure. Studies prove that it works. In a 1986 trial, premature babies given massage gained more weight, were more alert and active, and left hospital six days earlier than a control group. Babies who are massaged also show lower levels of the stress hormone cortisol. The following gentle massage works with the baby clothed: many newborns dislike being naked. If your baby seems distressed or hungry, offer a cuddle or feed instead.

1 Lie with your back raised on cushions. Place your baby on her front on your chest, head to one side. Gently stroke down her back from neck to buttocks with alternate horizontal palms, always keeping one hand in touch with her body.

2 When she seems relaxed, sit up, bend your knees, and place your baby on her back against your thighs. With the fingertips of both hands, stroke up from above the navel, sweeping out over the shoulders and down the arms and legs. Glide back up to the starting position and repeat the movement, keeping the stroke smooth and avoiding the umbilical area.

3 Finish by circling her palms and soles with your thumbs, gently cradling the hand or foot in your fingers.

How to stay happy

New motherhood is so overwhelming that you can lose yourself in its never-endingness. Here are ways to keep sane.

● **Find at least one attractive breastfeeding outfit:** dresses and skinny jeans are months off.

● **Buy great pajamas:** at night they open for easy nursing and keep shoulders and legs warm; during the day they discourage unwelcome visitors.

● **Congratulate yourself seven days on:** you survived the strangest week of your life and deserve more flowers, chocolates, and a cuddle.

● **Clear the chaos:** being surrounded by detritus saps the spirit.

● **Revel in the niceness:** choosing fantastic clothes for your baby distracts from the vomit and poop.

● **Smile and change the subject:** when asked "Doesn't she have a routine?" "She can't be hungry again?" or "What did you do today?"

● **Experience each day fully:** in four weeks' time you may only half-remember this strange newborn phase, and long to recapture it.

● **Give yourself a treat every day:** wash your hair, call a friend, have a lavender bath, eat cake.

● **Grab minutes for yourself:** make the most of babies who lie contentedly staring at a window.

● **Spoil yourself:** you deserve a little luxury. I satisfied a burning desire for ridiculously high Prada heels. Knowing I have the perfect shoes for glamorous, chauffeured nights out sipping cocktails, gives me hope.

Dealing with change

Motherhood puts us through immense upheaval. The secret of peace is having the flexibility to go with the flow. I didn't relax until my second birth, when I found that if I stopped controlling and refusing to compromise, motherhood became easier and I laughed more. Perhaps we can learn from Buddhism, which states that life is ever-changing, and best encountered through the detachment that meditation teaches. It's as easy as focusing on the matter in hand, without letting in the train of thoughts that make you feel dissatisfied, overwhelmed, or nostalgic for the past.

- **Lower your expectations:** aim to do just one particular thing a day. Maybe as little as making a wish list.

- **Stop anticipating:** don't worry about what happens next or how long the baby will sleep or feed. No two days will be the same for a while.

- **Focus on the big picture:** it can be a relief to recollect the fact that one day your baby will be five or eighteen; you won't be doing this forever. There is plenty to look forward to.

Switch-off meditation

1 Whatever you're doing, stop thinking and focus on that activity to the exclusion of all else. If feeding, look at your baby and witness his reactions to the milk, feel your arm cradling him; be filled with that connection.

2 Watch how your breathing naturally coordinates with your actions. When thoughts butt in, acknowledge them, sensing how they take the edge off your calm, then return to your focus.

Letting go

Many of us now don't become mothers until we're in our thirties. As daughters, we are brought up to believe we can achieve anything if we work for it, and this assumption, for many, leads to long, high-powered careers in which people do what we suggest. We set agendas, schedules, and budgets, and make them work. We hire and fire. We leave the house early in the morning and come home only when (and if) we want. Then comes motherhood. Suddenly we're not in charge. A tiny thing that can't walk or talk decides when (or if) we get dressed, when we eat or chat, whether we go out (probably not), and where (somewhere with child-friendly feeding rooms). Above all, it stops us sleeping. Resistance isn't the answer. By the birth of my third child, I finally got it: I should imagine I was a reckless student again for a few months, and everything would be fine—no set bedtime, no responsibilities, no deadlines that couldn't be extended, and no career plan. Long lie-ins and little afternoon snoozes; reading novels and watching daytime TV. Dashing from recently discovered coffee shop or gallery to tea at a new friend's apartment. I felt lost and out of my depth, but exhilarated by the sense of a new life unfolding, every relationship being reevaluated, and endless possibilities opening up.

I WAS MANIC ABOUT DOING EVERYTHING RIGHT. DON'T BE HARD ON YOURSELF AND EVERYTHING BECOMES EASIER.

Stacey, *mother of Betsi, 3, and Hank, 1 day.*

Feeling loss

All mothers crave their old carefree life. Weeks after giving birth, I found myself unexpectedly out on my own without the baby. In my purse were my credit card and passport. For a moment I considered buying a plane ticket to somewhere far away to find my "real" self again. Motherhood brings loss: of being a couple, of friendships that won't last the course, of lack of responsibilities, of being on your own. It's healthy to mourn your old life: moan about all the things you miss to a friend; shed some tears; rage out loud and feel better; or contemplate the words of the Buddha, "Cling not to that which changes." The sense of loss diminishes with time and as you discover the riches of your new role. And when you do, eventually, get a life again, you may feel a perverse sadness that your child is not there to share it.

Affirmation for loss

Try repeating this affirmation when you feel low to acknowledge these very normal feelings of loss and to help assuage the guilt that accompanies them: "Things change. I forgive myself for wanting things back as they were."

The monotony of servicing someone else got me down. I'd been used to managing a busy office, juggling several tasks at once with staff coming to me for advice. Suddenly all I had to juggle was washing up, feeding, and endless changing. And I wasn't making a good job of it.

Faith, *mother of Lateefah, 17 months.*

Tips for raising energy

You may feel you lack energy for months after the birth. When you feel you can't stay awake a second longer but have to keep on keeping on, try these quick fixes.

● **Take an energy eyebath:** rub your palms together briskly to generate heat. Rest them over your eye sockets, blocking out light without putting pressure on the eyes. Stare into the dark for a minute or so, trying not to blink. Remove your palms, then tap your fingers over your scalp, from the forehead to the base of the skull.

● **Salute the dawn:** sunrise is a great time to be awake. In India they say this is when energy is at its most concentrated, and meditation will focus energy for the day in the most beneficial way.

● **Nap during the day:** try and take advantage of when your baby sleeps.

● **Take a walk:** when your butt is numb from sitting to feed, put the baby in a sling and go for a walk. Breathe in fresh air and enjoy sunlight on your sleep-deprived skin.

● **Establish a routine:** if your baby sleeps all day only to wake when you're ready for bed, start following a calming bedtime routine (page 37).

Energy-reclamation visualization
Think of the energy you expend in feeding, bathing, wiping, carrying, and empathizing. Imagine gathering back this energy, pulling in shafts of light until you have a pulsating ball of energy inside. Feel the healing force of this energy, and reclaim it.

IN SOUTHERN NIGERIA YORUBA
MOTHERS DO NOTHING FOR TWO
MONTHS—NO WASHING, CLEANING,
COOKING; WE DON'T EVEN CHANGE THE
BABY—WE JUST LIE IN BED SLEEPING
AND FEEDING. NO ONE THERE GETS
DEPRESSED ABOUT PROBLEMS SLEEPING
OR BREASTFEEDING.

Stella, *mother of Temitope, 15, Temitayo, 12, and Oluwatosin, 11.*

2

Feeding

Breastfeeding

Breastfeeding should be the most natural activity in the world. It doesn't feel that way when you're struggling with bleeding nipples at the dead of night to satisfy an increasingly distressed babe who can't latch on. Breastfeeding is a skill you need to be taught one-to-one, and you have to be outspoken, determined, and persistent to get the information you need. So call that helpline, insist on a home visit from a nursing support counselor, and demand that the midwife shows you how to get the baby to latch on. When you are offered conflicting advice or are made to feel inadequate, try to remember that although it seems impossible now, in three months' time breastfeeding will make your life easy, and that it's the most important thing you can do to safeguard your own and your baby's health. Mothers who breastfeed are less likely to get breast cancer—for each year you feed, you cut your risk by 4.3 percent. For babies, nursing reduces the risk of allergies and infections, and boosts intelligence. It also forges a powerful emotional connection between you that means breastfed babies cry less. The downside, apart from the initial pain? Research shows that breastfed babies spend less time asleep and lying quietly on their own. And feeding on demand can mean nursing almost twenty-four hours a day at first.

After I discovered feeding lying down, I relaxed into night feeds.

Marina, *mother of Luisa, 8 months.*

Nursing tips

The secret of successful breastfeeding is to nurse as often and as long as your baby wants, and to resist giving formula, however enticing a baby who feeds quicker and sleeps longer.

● **Rest:** the more tired and upset you are, the less easy it is to nurse.

● **Get comfortable:** this is even more essential after a cesarean. Support your back, arm, and baby, with feet flat on the floor. Make sure you're warm, with entertainment to hand (remote control, phone, book, drink, snack).

● **Start over:** keep trying until the baby latches on well—body and head in line, nose to nipple, mouth open wide with lower lip pulled back, ears wiggling as she sucks.

● **Believe in yourself:** you almost certainly have enough milk. And the more often a well-latched-on infant feeds, the more you make.

● **Stay calm:** this may be hard when he's screaming for milk, but the letdown of milk comes more readily when you relax.

● **Breathe:** exhaling, relax shoulders away from ears, imagining your milk as a copious fountain or neverending thread.

● **Drink water:** you need at least 3½ pints (2 liters) daily. Cranberry juice is a good postbirth kidney/bladder cleanser.

● **Snack healthily:** for three months, add 300–400 calories to your regular healthy diet: apricots, nuts, seeds, and olives for easy vitamins; calcium-rich yogurts; egg, cheese, chicken, or mackerel salad on wholewheat bread for zinc and DHA. And 70 percent cocoa-solids chocolate…

Whiling away feedtime

Resign yourself to living on the couch for a few weeks. Some childcare authors argue that you should engage with your baby by looking at her while she feeds. Mothers might argue that after a week or so, this saps your will to live. Here are some other options.

● **Watch TV:** raid the video store for weepy chick flicks or movies your partner hates. Reruns of *ER* did it for me.

● **Stimulate your brain:** plow through everything you have meant to read since high school, learn a language, keep a diary, or use guidebooks to plan a holiday.

● **Keep in touch:** make calls (harder to do while feeding once the baby becomes more alert), write letters and thank-you cards.

● **Practice Kegel exercises:** dull but vital if you want to laugh or cough in years to come. They also prevent a numb butt during long feeds. Whenever you remember, pull in the muscles surrounding your anus. Hold, and release. Repeat twelve times. Then hold, pull in further, hold, then release. Repeat. Repeat with the muscles you use to stop yourself peeing. Natural birth guru Sheila Kitzinger suggests writing the words "Happy Birthday" with your pelvic floor muscles, dotting the "i" and crossing the "t"; try your name, too.

AFTER A COUPLE OF WEEKS, I WELCOMED THE CHANCE TO PUT MY FEET UP FOR HOURS, AND SURRENDERED TO DAYTIME TV. WHEN I REALLY NEEDED TO DO SOMETHING, I PUT HIM IN THE SLING.

Lisa, *mother of Jack, 4 months.*

Nonstop feeding

Some breastfed babies try a killer tactic: they start feeding at 5pm, and, switching from breast to breast, can still be there at midnight. My breastfeeding counselor suggested that I regard the feed as a multicourse French meal and retire to bed with a glass of red wine, cheese, and biscuits, so that baby and I could indulge in some sort of crazed cheese and wine party. It may also help to feed on one side for an hour, and wind well before switching. With my third baby, I found that if I fed her in the dark for an hour, placed her in the crib and left, she'd sleep. And I got an evening. Whatever your strategy, console yourself with the thought that this stage doesn't last more than a few weeks.

Relief for tense shoulders

This yoga stretch stimulates the thyroid—the poor functioning of which has been linked with postnatal depression. Alternatively, ask for a massage of small, circular thumb pressures over the sides of the neck, shoulders, and shoulderblades.

1 Bring shoulders to ears as you inhale. Hold the breath, squeezing tightly. Release on the exhalation. Repeat.

2 Exhaling, take your chin down and in toward your throat. Squeeze. Inhaling, pivot to point your chin at the ceiling. Swallow 7 times.

3 Drop left ear to left shoulder. Feel the stretch at the base of the spine. Repeat on the right. Inhaling, pivot to look left. Exhale and look behind. Repeat to the right.

4 Make large circles with your head clockwise, then counterclockwise. Work slowly at tense points.

Introducing solids

New mothers race to this momentous point, desperate to take babies to the next stage. Experienced mothers seem less hasty, in the knowledge that weaning means carrying around tiny pots of puréed mush and breadsticks that mess up your purse. In the West this special time for mothers has no greater significance to the wider community, but it is an opportunity for advertisers to sell us babyfood and other paraphernalia. To HIndus, the first taste of solid food is so special that it forms the seventh of sixteen sacred sacraments— rites of passage that sanctify the body, purify the soul, and cultivate virtuous behavior from babyhood onward. This ceremony—*annaprasana*—takes place no earlier than the child's sixth or seventh month, and sometimes not until first teeth have erupted after this point; research corroborates that breastmilk or formula contains everything an infant needs until then. On the day of the ritual, guests gather and exchange gifts, a silver bowl and spoon are brought out, and photographs mark the occasion. The first food comprises a little well-cooked rice that is blended with ghee (clarified butter) to bring fame and brilliance, or yogurt and honey. Sacred mantras are chanted. The bowl is offered to a sacred flame over which herbs are burned to supplicate the goddess of speech and vigor. Prayers are said to request that the child might be strong, well-spoken, and long-lived. The father then invites the child to taste, stating "Master this first meal and your body will be strong." Everyone eats and drinks in celebration.

Feeding and independence

You can't keep doing everything for your baby. To sense why she might want to feed herself, have someone feed lunch to you. Do you get what you want, when you want? If you don't believe your baby can feed herself, give her a bowl of cereal, milk, and a spoon. Cover the floor with a plastic sheet and look away if you must. The satisfaction when she gets some in compensates for the mess. Here are ways to tempt newly independent eaters and toddlers.

● **Serve food in several different bowls:** this counters the boredom that means "bowl on the floor."

● **After some weeks, go back to a single bowl:** innovation, innovation.

● **Keep the brain occupied:** picking up peas, corn kernels, or garbanzo beans one by one is fascinating.

● **Make a picnic:** lay a cloth and paper plates (until they crawl).

● **Serve a healthy dessert:** when kids start to flag, offer fruit, yogurt, or rice pudding and see how appetites return.

● **Eat together:** adults and kids sharing the same meal? So unusual in some homes that children laugh in amazement.

● **Think like a child:** in our kitchen spaghetti is worms, broccoli is trees, and mushrooms are fairy houses.

● **Be more adventurous:** a hospital nutritionist advised a friend to serve meals in interesting receptacles—she resorted to a boat and an envelope.

● **Don't react:** even one-year-olds derive pleasure from a mother wound up about binning another lovingly prepared meal that has been refused.

Great first foods

Babies of six months are curious about food. When a little hand grabs toast off your plate, it may be time for solids. Organic baby rice mixed with your baby's regular milk is a good starter—begin by offering it once a day after a short milk feed. Once your baby accepts this happily, introduce more interesting selections: experiment with combinations, freezing them in an ice tray for instant meals. The more variety your baby tries in the first six months, the more open he will be to taste sensations thereafter. If he spits out food or turns his head away, don't fret: try again in a week or so. Choose organic ingredients.

APPLE AND PEAR PURÉE

I apple   I pear

Peel, deseed, and finely chop the apple and pear, then simmer the fruit in a little water until soft. For very young babies, strain to remove stringy fibers.

BANANA AND MANGO PURÉE

I large banana   I mango

Peel the banana and mango, then blitz the flesh in a food processor. Strain to remove fibers. After a couple of weeks' happy feeding, stir in natural yogurt.

SWEET POTATO AND CARROT PURÉE

| I red-fleshed sweet potato | I large carrot |

Peel dice the vegetables. Simmer in a little water until soft. Mash with a fork. For a very young baby, press the purée through a strainer.

 ### POTATO AND PEA PURÉE

| I potato | a little butter |
| I handful fresh or frozen peas | baby's regular milk |

Peel and dice the potato. Simmer with the peas in a little water until soft. Strain for very young babies, or mash with butter and milk. After a few weeks' happy feeding, try grating Parmesan cheese on top for extra taste and nutritional value.

3

I WISH I'D HAD THE CONFIDENCE TO BE MORE RUTHLESS ABOUT THE SLEEPING WHEN SHE WAS A FEW MONTHS OLD; IT'S MUCH HARDER NOW SHE CAN WALK AND TALK.

Gabrielle, *mother of Minnie, 18 months.*

Sleeping

Sound sleeping

Few babies and toddlers sleep as soundly or as long as their exhausted mothers would wish. For months babies wake every few hours for milk, then just when they seem to be feeding less often and sleeping more reliably, teething kicks in to disrupt the pattern. Most mothers of young children endure months without an uninterrupted night's sleep. When it's impossible to catch up with lie-ins and afternoon naps, exhaustion can become all-encompassing, preventing us from stringing together a sentence, let alone being the perfect mom. Not sleeping reduces immunity and robs us of the time that body and mind require to heal, repair, and process information. It makes us irritable and tearful, and is linked to postnatal depression. Children need deep, uninterrupted sleep, too. To deprive them of it by letting them stay up until they seem tired (some never do) is unkind. Successful parenting is about feeling confident enough to take control and establish that you are in charge, not your child. Teaching a child how to go to sleep and remain asleep is possible, and is one of the most empowering skills you can pass on as a mother. Everyone behaves better when they sleep through the night every night.

Bedtime routine

Children don't naturally acquire the knack of going to bed. For those of us who like to have an evening to ourselves, to spend time with a partner, on chores, or even working, it makes sense to establish a routine that lulls children into sleep. If you start this routine while a baby is young, he'll continue to settle to sleep easily when he is older.

- **Mealtime:** naturopaths often advise feeding a child foods rich in substances that cause the body to make serotonin, a sleep-inducing brain chemical. These sunstances include tryptophan, calcium, and vitamin B, found in foods such as bananas, milk, yogurt, cheese, and lettuce sandwiches (yes, some kids will eat lettuce).

- **Play:** boisterous enough to work off a child's energy.

- **Bathtime:** very calming; follow with a relaxing massage (page 41).

- **Story:** make sure it's not too exciting, and not too frightening.

- **Drink:** breastfeed or give warm milk, then supervise the brushing of teeth.

- **Cuddles:** combine with a song or bedtime music (see page 38).

- **Exit:** leave the room, then, if after 3 minutes, your child is crying, go in, briefly comfort her, then leave. Repeat, increasing the time you spend outside the room. This might take three hours the first night, twenty minutes the next, and by the third day, no time at all.

- **Routine:** repeat every night at the same time. Follow the routine and children will start begging for bed.

Tunes for bedtime

Music can soothe a baby to sleep. Baby sleep tapes are used in some 8,000 hospitals and babycare centers across North America. In some states hospitals send new mothers home with a CD specially compiled to stimulate the growing mind and combat constant crying and sleeplessness. Studies of premature babies show that those exposed to music have boosted oxygen levels, weight gain, sucking ability, and head circumference (a sign of intelligence). Music also reduces pain—research has revealed an auditory neural pathway running from the ear to the part of the brain associated with pain inhibition.

Look for compilations of sleep-inducing classical music, womb sounds, or ocean waves, which run for twenty minutes or longer, to pacify your child after you leave the room, or try my children's favorites below. Even better, make your own music, singing lullabies or humming gently with your lips on the side of your baby's head—what baby-massage instructors call "sonic massage."

Music for sleepy babies

Steve Reich *Six Marimbas* (Nonesuch): sixteen minutes of gradual changes anchored by calming undertones.

Raymond Scott *Soothing Sounds for Baby* (search secondhand vinyl stores): age-graded sonic experimentation that babies love (sounds strange to adults).

Terry Riley *Descending Moonshine Dervishes* (Kuck Kuck): rippling layers of waves that dissolve time.

The Abyssinians and Friends *Tree of Satta* (Blood and Fire): twenty versions of roots reggae's most spiritual anthem.

Cosy bedroom

At the end of the day a welcoming nursery encourages sleep. Tidy up together to create calm vibes and space at the center of the room, thought in Vaastu (Indian feng shui) to be important in evoking feelings of comfort and security.

● **Soothing scent:** place a drop of essential oil of lavender or camomile in the water-filled bowl of a vaporizer and light the candle.

● **Darkness:** fix blackout roller blinds beneath drapes to keep the nursery dark, especially in summer. Children really do wake later in a darkened room. Try to wean babies away from nightlights: body and eyes need complete darkness every twenty-four hours to rebalance and repair.

● **All tucked up in bed:** when an experienced mother told me to sew flaps on the long sides of my one-year-old's quilt cover, I was astounded. Was she a Stepford Wife? But it works: if you make the flaps 1ft (30cm) wide, you can tuck your baby in so well that he can't kick the covers off and so will sleep longer.

● **Baby sleeping bags:** copy French, German, and Dutch mothers and use a well-fitting baby sleeping bag instead of blankets, sheets, and quilts, once your baby is over six weeks old. Zip your baby in and, whichever way he turns, he can't escape and get chilled. Dutch studies suggest that baby sleeping bags are the safest form of bedding because they prevent infants from pulling covers over their heads and sliding beneath blankets (avoiding a risk of suffocation), and stop toddlers climbing.

Soothing a baby to sleep

In Papua New Guinea, mothers suspend babies from the rafters of a house in a *bilum*, a hammock-like string bag, for daytime naps. In the breeze, protected from animals and insects, babies rock themselves into slumber. Try a baby hammock (suitable for infants up to nine months) for naptimes, or, more luxuriously, climb into a hammock together and see how the rhythm soothes you both to sleep—the perfect summer snooze. But for evening bedtime some of the following ideas might do the trick.

● **Third-eye massage:** Many Eastern medicines and religions recognize a series of seven invisible energy centers, or chakras, within the body. The brow chakra is also known as the third eye. To massage it, gently circle the area between the eyebrows with your middle finger. Babies look puzzled, then drift into another world, eventually to sleep.

● **Reinforcements:** to break a spell of bad nights, ask a grandmother or good friend to "do" bedtime. Sometimes babies behave impeccably with people they're not used to walking all over.

● **Lavender bath:** dilute 1 drop of essential oil of lavender in 1 tsp sweet almond oil and add to a bath, swishing to disperse before placing your baby in it.

● **Camomile bath:** make a pot of camomile tea using three teabags and leave to infuse for ten minutes. Pour into the bath and check the temperature before bathing your child. For children over two, supplement by offering a little cooled camomile tea at bedtime, sweetened with honey if desired.

Calming massage

Babies love having their legs and feet rubbed, so this massage makes a comforting inclusion in a bedtime routine. Ensure the room is warm (80°F or 26°C), and stop if your baby cries or seems too hungry or tired to enjoy the attention. Apply a little sweet almond oil to your hands before you start.

Caution: *before using oil, do a patch test—dab a little on the skin and wait twenty-four hours to see if it causes redness or irritation.*

1 Place your baby on her back, with her legs and feet exposed. Sit in front of her feet. Wrap your left hand around the back of her left thigh. Gently pull down the upper and the lower leg, releasing pressure at the knee. As your hand reaches the ankle, repeat the sequence with your right hand, building a smooth flow of strokes, and alternating between hands.

2 Take the left foot in one hand, the calf in the other, and rotate the ankle clockwise, then counterclockwise.

3 Sandwich the foot between your hands. Stroke your top hand down the upper part of the foot and away at the toes. Repeat in a flowing movement.

4 Cup the top of the foot with your fingers and rub one thumb, then the other, up the sole and out beneath the toes in a T-shape. Build up a rhythm.

5 Squeeze each toe from base to tip, then rotate the digit and pull away at the tip. Repeat all the steps on your baby's right leg and foot.

Night waking

We all wake naturally during the night. The different phases of human sleep include a brief waking in which we check that all is as it should be before drifting off again. Adults are hardly aware of this. But for babies who go to sleep in the arms of a carer, to wake alone in a crib is frightening; it's only natural that they wail. Teaching your child to go to sleep on his own—teaching that life is safe without you—is one of the hardest tasks of motherhood because it starts the separation process. An infant over six months does not need night feeds for nutrition. However tempting it is to offer breast or bottle for instant peace and quiet, it's better for your long-term sanity and energy levels to set a bedtime routine (page 37) and teach sleeping skills now. Once children can walk and talk, it's many times more difficult.

An effective approach

1 When your child wakes, wait a few minutes; he may settle naturally.

2 If not, go to him, offer a cuddle and reassuring words, but resist a story, feed, rocking, or a trip to your bed.

3 After a few minutes, tuck him in, say goodnight, and leave.

4 If he cries, wait 30 seconds, then go to him. Offer comfort, but leave.

5 If he continues to cry, repeat step 4, doubling the time between visits. Although this can tug at the heartstrings, by the third or fourth night, many infants will sleep through. You just have to remain firm in your resolve.

Coping with sleepless nights

Life is hell when you haven't had a full night's sleep or a dream for months. Try these reviving solutions the morning after a terrible night.

● **Refreshing aromatherapy bath:** run a tepid bath and, just before stepping in, add 5 drops essential oil of lemon or 4 drops each essential oils of mandarin and grapefruit. Swish to disperse, then close your eyes for five minutes, if possible, while the vapors revive and invigorate. Avoid direct sunlight for six hours afterward: these oils can cause skin photosensitivity.

● **Foot massage:** for physical and mental tiredness, add 4 drops essential oil of rosemary to 1 tbsp sweet almond oil and then use to massage the feet. To deal with exhaustion, substitute 3 drops each essential oils of clary sage and lavender.

● **Bonding:** find someone in the same situation, turn up on the doorstep to sob over coffee and chocolate cake, exchange confessions, and laugh at the impossibleness of it all.

● **Help:** find someone to look after the baby for an hour or two while you sleep—it can make all the difference. Do swaps with another mom.

● **Yoga eye exercises:** keeping your head still and trying not to blink, look up, hold, then down. Look left, hold, then right. Look left up, hold, then right down. Look right up, hold, then left down. Repeat five times.

● **Morning mantra:** recite Julian of Norwich's words—"But all shall be well, and all shall be well, and all manner of things shall be well." Try to invest faith in these words.

4

THE WORST PART OF MOTHERHOOD
IS HEARING HER CRY AND NOT
KNOWING HOW TO MAKE IT BETTER.

Georgia, *mother of Ava, 16 months.*

Crying

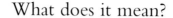

What does it mean?

It takes a while to be able to interpret the significance of the tiny variations in a baby's crying that denote boredom, pain, hunger, and discomfort. And the misery of not understanding is one of the most upsetting issues of early motherhood. The more time you spend with your baby tending to her everyday needs, the easier it gets; and the more confidently you respond to her, the more love grows. Baby yoga can help: because it stimulates every body system, from the digestive system to the nervous system, plus circulatory and immune functions, it can alleviate specific problems, from colicky crying to constipation, while allowing you and your baby to relax and settle in each other's company. When the crying gets too much, put your baby safely in a crib, leave the room, and try to get away from the wailing for five minutes. Close your eyes and imagine your child aged five, fifteen, or fifty. Contemplate how different life will be then. Acquiring a sense of perspective can offer comfort.

Soothing fractious babies

Babies seem to get restless and resist collapsing contentedly onto the couch at the very time you need to do just that—at the end of a long day. When your baby won't settle in the evening, these ideas may help.

● **Move rooms:** babies can get bored with being in the same space for hours. Just moving from kitchen to bathroom can help.

● **Use a bouncy chair:** park the chair in front of the washing machine and put a load of clothes in to wash. The sounds and movement often mesmerize babies.

● **Turn on the vacuum cleaner:** a gushing faucet works as well, or tune in a radio to "white noise."

● **Play classical music:** Bach can be particularly soothing for its repetition and counterpoint.

● **Walk the baby around:** show him pictures on the wall—mine liked black-and-white photographs and the geometric patterns of a patchwork quilt.

● **Carry the baby in a sling:** get on with mindless chores; picking up toys is good.

● **Put the baby down:** sometimes they're just sick of being played with.

● **Test if it's "leave me alone" crying:** some babies seem prone to this after a day's handling, stimulation, and feeding. All they may need is a brief spell alone in a crib followed by a sleepy feed in the dark to ease into slumber.

Colicky crying

When a baby is well, but cries inconsolably every evening, pulling up her legs in pain, she may be diagnosed with "colic," a condition that still baffles the medical establishment. It tends to come on when a baby is aged between one and three months, and usually disappears as spontaneously as it arrives. Some mothers have come up with ideas—why not give them a try?

● **Rocking and movement:** go for a walk with the sling or stroller; as a last resort, strap the baby into an infant seat in the back of the car and take a drive.

● **Trigger foods:** some babies seem sensitive to cabbage and other cruciferous vegetables, caffeine, dairy products, and citrus fruit in mother's milk. Keep a food diary to check, then exclude possible culprits for a day or two to see if it makes a difference.

● **Flying angel hold:** try this holding position (page 69).

● **Sonic massage:** place your lips on your baby's head or chest and vibrate the word *"Om"* (pronounced Aaa Oom Mmm) onto her body.

● **Baths:** bath together (page 58).

● **Fennel tea:** steep one organic teabag in a mug of boiling water for five minutes. Once it is cool, offer a little on a sterilized baby spoon. Or bring a teaspoon of fennel seeds to boil in a cup of your baby's regular milk, simmer for five minutes, strain, and add a little to a bottle.

Action cures for colic

Baby yoga and massage offer effective relief for the intestinal spasms that may be a factor in colic. At the very least, these therapies distract you and your baby from the hell of constant evening crying, and give parents something positive and active to do to ease their baby's distress.

Gentle abdominal massage

1 After a diaper change, look at your baby and explain what you are going to do. Warm your hands, dab a little sweet almond oil on your fingertips, and gently rest them on your baby's abdomen.

2 Working carefully, gently circle the navel in a clockwise direction with both hands. Let one hand complete a whole circle, while the other makes a half circle, lifting it over the first hand when they meet. Work rhythmically, gradually taking the circles wider and wider to cover the whole abdominal region. Talk to your baby as you massage him; show him how confident you are.

Baby yoga routine

1 With your baby lying on his back, diaper removed, look him in the eyes, smile, and explain what you're going to do. Take his lower legs in each hand.

2 Push his knees toward his stomach and apply gentle pressure. Hold briefly, then release. Repeat a few times.

3 Place the soles of his feet together so the knees fall outward, and, without moving his hips, circle the legs clockwise, then counterclockwise.

4 Stretch the legs toward you, pulling slightly and then dropping, saying "relax" as you do so.

Teething

Cutting teeth hurts babies. For months before teeth erupt in that gummy mouth, infants suffer. Signs include a red cheek and constant dribble, frequent yellow diapers and diaper rash (experts claim this is unrelated; mothers beg to differ), fretful crying, clinging, and refusal to eat. The wakeful nights that accompany symptoms can blight the entire household. The bad news is that teething troubles persist until the last molars emerge, usually before the age of three. Here are some potential solutions.

- **Textured teethers:** corduroy and a damp washcloth are good textures for biting on, and don't hurt sore gums.

- **Apple teether:** chill a segment of apple and tie in muslin; healthier than chewing a plastic teething ring.

- **Sore gums:** rub with a finger; even babies who won't usually let you near the mouth go all dreamy.

- **Homeopathic remedies:** try Chamomilla 6x for distressed babies, Aconite 6c for feverish pain, Pulsatilla 6c for clingy tearfulness. These may be more effective than cure-all homeopathic teething remedies sold in drugstores.

- **Acupressure point:** take the web of skin between your child's thumb and index finger between your thumb and index finger. Apply pressure and hold for a few seconds before releasing.

- **Gum rub:** for infants over one year, stir 1 drop essential oil of clove into 1 tsp pasteurized honey and rub on.

Toddler tantrums

In my experience, "terrible twos" start just after a child's first birthday and last until they're almost four. Tantrums are supremely effective in public—supermarket, baby clinic, birthday party—when other adults are around to tut disapprovingly. Here are strategies to silence the shrieks and foot stamping.

● **Don't react:** ignore where possible. In a supermarket find an interesting shelf to peruse and edge away. Ignore the stares of other shoppers.

● **Distract:** this can be draining but effective. Discover a particularly fun toy in your bag and play with it, sing a song, or stand on your head.

● **Use humor:** when you can't reason, use the mime artist's repertoire—funny face, talking without sound coming out, silly walk. I've known strangers to join in at the checkout.

● **Get the timing right:** don't go to places where kids are expected to behave when you are both tired or hungry. Tantrums seem worse when you both need a snack or a nap.

● **Be proud of your child's spirit:** "naughty" children can be the most creative, lively, and fun to be around.

● **Praise cooperative behavior:** appeal to his instinct to be liked.

● **Give responsibility:** even youngsters of eighteen months can be in charge of choosing apples, picking out carrots, or selecting a special cake while shopping. Ivory Coast mothers sometimes give young children freedom that ensures they conform: a mother might walk down the street without looking back, expecting the child to follow.

Staying patient

When your toddler has climbed on the table, emptied the sugar bowl on the floor, then thrown herself off for the tenth time that morning, it's easy to forget that small children learn by perpetually exploring, experimenting, and testing out new experiences, and that it's vital for their development to push the boundaries and see where the limits are. When you can't contact your feelings of loving motherliness and a child prevents you from escaping from their world even for a momentary phone call, try these ideas.

Composed breathing

1 Close your eyes. Inhale to the count of 4, retain the breath for a count of 4, then exhale to the count of 4.

2 Repeat the breathing technique for 2–3 minutes, or as long as it takes to ease your disquiet. As you inhale, imagine peace filling you. While you hold the breath, feel your sense of inner calm expanding. As you slowly exhale, visualize mental and emotional toxins being expelled with the carbon dioxide.

Meditation for equanimity

Make sure your child is away from potential danger, get out the photo album, then sit quietly and witness the transient nature of time by looking at some photographs of your child from a few months ago. Remember the things she did then that sent you crazy, and see how many problems have resolved themselves with time. Gaining distance from the present gives a widened perspective that builds a sense of patience and future possibilities.

Anger management

Looking after young children day in and day out is brain-meltingly boring. Crying babies make you want to run away; clingy toddlers suffocate. The accompanying guilt can cause raging anger. On a good morning I'm Perfect Mom, serving up fresh fruit and oatmeal, slipping the kids good-humoredly into clean clothes that I set out the night before, listening to my eldest read while I jiggle the baby on my knee. After a sleepless night, I'm a snarling hellhound, chucking additive-loaded breakfast cereal at the table while emptying the washing basket on the floor in search of a T-shirt that can be worn once more. Time for a break.

● **Allow one more DVD or cookie:** you need a ten-minute break to clear your head.

● **Put your child in the crib:** leave the room and act like your inconsolable baby or tantrummy toddler. Beat the pillow, sob, and ask for a cuddle.

● **Explore the feeling:** sense how anger comprises tiny shreds of guilt, desire, loss, and pain. Let the sensations disperse peacefully, forgiving the child, situation, and yourself. See how anger and love are intertwined.

● **Take a step back:** witness the effects anger has on your body—increased breathing and temperature, fluttering stomach—this alone can calm.

● **Harness the energy:** channel your anger into a furious aerobics session with the children, scream along to heavy metal music, dig the garden furiously.

● **Explain and apologize:** kids will then see that anger is normal, that we all make mistakes, and that feelings can be resolved by talking and asking for forgiveness.

5

> IN GERMANY WE DO EVERYTHING
> NATURALLY, PREFERRING PLAIN
> WATER TO LOTIONS; I EVEN
> BLOW-DRIED MY BABY'S BOTTOM!
>
> **Anya,** *mother of Genua, 5.*

Bathing

Cleaning power of water

Babies don't need a bath every day. But some love it so much that it becomes not an opportunity for cleansing, but a chance to have fun. The best fun of all comes, of course, when you climb in too, to chat, play, and soak fully engaged in your child's activities. In places where people use sweating to cleanse the body—Turkey, Russia, Finland, Mexico, and Guatemala—new mothers may visit the baths for a cleansing ritual some seven to forty days following birth. Traditionally, many women will have given birth in this very place. Finland's smoke sauna, for instance, was in the past perhaps the only warm, sterile environment with plenty of hot water in a village. It was also a place of dark, quiet privacy, conducive to the beginning of the birthing process. The return to this bathing space might help women reflect on the birth, coming to terms with difficulties and reliving the joys. Incorporating pampering baths into your postbirth recovery program not only revives the body, it lightens the spirit.

Caution: *never leave a baby or child alone in the bath, even for a few seconds. Gather everything you need before you start (towel, diaper, shampoo). If the phone or doorbell rings, ignore it or take the infant with you to answer it.*

Baths for new mothers

The early weeks after birth are in many cultures a time for cleansing as well as resting. Find time for these relaxing options.

● **Breastfeeding bath:** run a warm bath. Just before stepping in, add 6 drops essential oil of fennel or 10 drops essential oil of geranium, swishing to disperse. These oils are renowned for increasing the flow of milk.

● **Nursing bath:** climb into a warm, deep bath to feed a fractious baby. Water calms crying infants and stressed mothers alike. Have someone top up the warm water as it cools.

● **Steam bath:** in Turkey, babies are traditionally taken to the hammam baths on the fortieth day after birth for a ritual of cleansing, song, and feasting. A deep-heat treatment is a nice way to mark the end of the early weeks. After your six-week check, have someone look after the baby while the intense heat of a sauna or steam room relaxes every muscle and cleanses your mind for 20 minutes. Follow with a refreshing shower, then a feast in a restaurant with family, friends, and baby.

● **Meditation bath:** take a long, hot, candlelit bath to contemplate the birth, and imprint special moments on your memory while they are still fresh.

Bathing together

Bathtime for new babies is scary. Rather than fussing around with slippery plastic baby baths, climb into the tub yourself, and have someone hand your baby to you. You'll both feel more secure and relaxed. And what could be better for bonding than such face-to-face, skin-to-skin contact? Bathing together can be an early-evening lifesaver when everyone's in a bad mood—you can relax and it cheers a cranky child.

Bathtime for young babies

1 Step into the bath and check the temperature (it should be tepid body temperature). Ask someone to pass your baby to you. Talk and smile as you lower him into the water with a cuddle. If he cries, try feeding him to make him feel comfortable.

2 Bend your knees and rest your baby's back against your thighs. Slowly lower him into the water, cupping the back of his head in one hand, his lower back in the other. Move him gently away through the water and back toward you, singing and maintaining eye contact.

3 When your baby seems at ease, rest his back against your chest, his bottom in your lap and move first his arms, then his legs up and down in the water: play splashing games. Talk and sing as you play. Finish the bath before he seems tired.

AT THE END OF THE DAY WHEN I CAN'T STAND UP ANY LONGER, WE RELAX IN THE BATH TOGETHER. THEN SHE POOPS ON ME.

Stephanie, *mother of Chloë, 18 months.*

Water confidence for older babies

Once your baby can sit unaided in the bath, the fun really starts, especially if you're in the tub, too. The confidence these bath games instill is the first step toward making swimming a happy experience. When your child gets cold or bored, lift her out and wrap her in a huge warm fluffy towel for a cuddle.

● **Throwing and catching:** lob balls or float ducks to each other.

● **Showering:** if you don't have a detachable showerhead, fill a large plastic pot with water, and tip it over your (and your baby's) back, knees, and heads.

● **Water pistols:** blast each other with squirty toys.

● **Bathtime picnic:** prepare "drinks" with a plastic tea set.

● **Dolly laundry:** wash dolls and their clothes, shampooing their hair.

● **Subaqua singing:** put your lips in the water to blow bubbles and sing.

● **Bouncing games:** sit children on your knees and "drop" them in the water, or play Row the Boat, See-saw, or Horsey Horsey.

Language bath
Bathing together is an excellent stimulus for language development—one of the few times when your face is at the level of your infant's for a sustained period (in the bath you can't escape to chores). Teach her to blow bubbles and play with the slippery soap, chatting and listening to the gurgles of delight. Ask questions and wait a little longer than usual for a response, which might come as a splash or smile rather than a word.

Baby swimming

If your child is happy and relaxed in the bath, capitalize on his ease and book some swimming classes. A young infant (from three months or so) is far easier to get into the water than an older toddler whose sense of fear and hatred of strangers has kicked in (remember, toddler tantrums are difficult to deal with in water with an audience). Studies of babies partaking in parent-involved swimming courses show that they have increased intelligence, concentration, and physical skills: swimming builds muscle tone and coordination, lung capacity, and gross motor skills. Being in water is positively liberating for many babies. Awkwardly static on land, gain the ability to propel themselves forward in the weightless aquatic environment. This will boost their self-awareness and their confidence, and introduce a joy in independence that sets them up for future achievements. If you are in the water with your child, letting go and catching on cue, will mean his sense of security gets a boost, too. You get to see how your child's personality responds to learning situations, which helps later in gearing activities to suit his temperament. It also teaches you how humor, play, and your own sense of enthusiasm augment the learning process. And then there are the safety benefits of learning to swim; remember that drowning is the second most common cause of death for under-fives in the United States.

Postbath massage

This time is perfect for massage. Your baby is warm and tired from splashing, her skin is moist and ready to absorb oil, and it induces the relaxation essential for sleep. You will need 1 tbsp sweet almond oil.

1 Make sure that the room is warm. Place your baby on her back on a warm towel. Kneel or sit in front of her feet. Smile and talk to her.

2 Warm some oil between your palms, then place your fingers on your baby's hips. Stroke up her torso and out over the shoulders. Glide down the arms to your starting position and repeat, building a steady rhythm.

3 Cupping the back of her left arm with one hand, slide your hand from her underarm to wrist. Repeat with your other hand. Repeat over and over, alternating you hands.

4 Take the back of her hand in your palm. With your thumb, stroke the palm, stretching the fingers. Gently rotate each finger, squeezing lightly at the tip. Repeat on the right arm and hand.

5 Repeat steps 3 and 4 on the legs and feet. Turn your baby onto her front (if she finds this strange, keep it brief). Repeat step 1, working from hips to shoulders.

6 Finish by placing your right palm on your baby's right shoulder. Stroke diagonally down the back and left leg to the foot. As you lift away at the foot, stroke your left hand from left shoulder to right foot. Build a continuous motion.

Baby dangling—a Nigerian tradition

Midwives may gasp, and you might not want to try this at home, but Nigerian mothers are taught by their own mothers how to give babies a vigorous postbath massage and workout before feeding them, morning and evening. This is said to strengthen the baby's limbs, enhance mobility, promote vital good health and alertness, and keep away colic. If you would like to experiment with the technique, keep your baby's bodyweight safely supported by placing one hand beneath his buttocks during the dandling.

1 A washcloth is soaked in hot water and wrung out. It is then used to massage the baby's muscles—on the arms and legs, abdomen and back—and joints, especially the knees and toes.

2 The mother holds the baby's hands and dandles him, allowing his bodyweight to stretch the limbs. She throws him in the air and catches him three times.

3 The mother holds one of the baby's hands and dandles him, moving the arm to swing the baby. She repeats with the other hand.

4 She takes the baby's arm behind his back, guides the hand between the shoulderblades, and holds. She repeats with the other arm.

5 The mother bends one of the baby's leg at the knee to take his foot to his buttocks. She holds, then repeats on the other leg.

6 The baby is briefly held upside down by the ankles.

Green diapering

Washable diapers mean less diaper rash, no chemicals or absorbable gels next to the skin, and no expense after the initial outlay. Infants who wear washable diapers tend to have fewer problems with potty training, since they know what a wet diaper feels like. These diapers can also make you feel very virtuous.

Look for shaped diapers that have a soft, breathable texture and fasten with Velcro, and use with a biodegradable liner so you can simply flush away the messy stuff. It's best to start when your baby is a few weeks old, when you feel a little more capable, and the baby is large enough to fit the diaper and not have leaks because of gaps. Try also the following natural cures for diaper rash.

● **A break from diapers:** take the diaper off and let your baby run bare for a while.

● **Massage blend:** add 3 drops essential oil of camomile to 1 tbsp sweet almond oil and massage into the diaper area after a bath.

● **Herbal creams:** look for those that use German camomile, pot marigold, lavender, and tea tree extracts to soothe reddened skin.

● **Diaper rinse:** add 3 drops essential oil of tea tree to the final rinse when washing diapers.

IT SOUNDS VAIN, BUT WHEN I SEE A LINE OF DIAPERS DRYING IN THE SUN, I FEEL LIKE A REAL MOM.

Susan, *mother of Carrie, 3 months*

6

A WALK WAS AN INSTANT CALMER,
LITERALLY, A BREATH OF FRESH AIR.
AS HE GOT OLDER, WALKS AROUND THE
FIELDS BECAME COFFEE MORNINGS,
WHICH BROUGHT THEIR OWN BENEFITS,
BUT I'VE NEVER FORGOTTEN THOSE
EARLY SPRINGTIME WALKS, WHEN IT
WAS JUST THE TWO OF US.

Joanna, *mother of Thomas, 6.*

Moving around

Welcome to the world

After a few weeks, babies start to uncurl, and with this new alertness comes a desire to experience the world. This tends to coincide with the end of the lying-in period, that special time when you welcome being sealed in a cocoon with your baby. During the lying-in month observed in China, mothers are discouraged from walking for fear of a sagging stomach, misaligned spine, and displaced joints. Eventually, though, it's time to emerge from hibernation and take a walk to introduce your baby to the natural world and her community. In Christian countries lying-in traditionally culminated in "churching," a service of welcome to the new mother and child.

As babies get older, they need to be outdoors daily; you can use this opportunity to meet people. My best friends are the happy result of desperate afternoon strolls around my neighborhood in search of someone who'd understand the strange things happening to me. Getting out and about helps combat the friendless invisibility that shrouds the early days of motherhood, when you belong neither to the world of your past nor to the new world of mothers who seem to know what they're doing.

The first venture outdoors

It can be unnerving to leave the house with a new baby for the first time. Cars seem faster than before, strangers and dogs menacingly unpredictable, the air polluted; and then there's that sling to struggle with and the fear that he'll need to nurse in public. But to show a tiny child the sun, sea, and trees for the first time is very special and worth turning into a family ritual. The first outing is one of Hinduism's sixteen sacred sacraments. In the fourth month after birth, the child is bathed, and dressed in special clothes, then taken outside just after sunrise and shown the sun for a few seconds with the words, "You are born of my body. May you outlive me and enjoy one hundred Falls" or a prayer to the sun, "May you bring brightness into the life of this child." Friends and relatives gather back at the house for a celebratory breakfast. That evening, the child is again dressed in new clothes and taken out to see the moon. The mother offers water to the moon in both palms and allows it to trickle to the ground while both parents pray for the child to enjoy a long and healthy life. You might like to adapt some of these ideas to create your own ceremony; parents across the world often plant a tree at this stage to grow and flourish with the child.

Places to go

Are you new to your neighborhood in the daytime? Many working women have a dormitory-like relationship with their home patch, and so lack things to do and people to see when a baby forces them outdoors every day. Here are some things to do locally.

● **Parent and baby group:** surprise yourself with how many friends you make. Mothers with slightly older babies can offer vital information and support when you feel lost. I found Sue, whose children were exactly a year older, and just copied what she did.

● **Postnatal yoga:** more for the after-class cookies and chat than exercise, since the babies inevitably cry and disrupt the proceedings.

● **Baby swim, gym, massage:** for an instant community of new mothers.

● **Baby clinic:** worth going to just to chat with another adult. But avoid it if you feel undermined or bullied.

● **Park or city farm:** if your baby is too young for swings, the café is a magnet for bored parents.

● **Café and coffee shop:** sample until you find those with the best cakes that are the most feeding-friendly.

● **Museums and galleries:** empty during weekdays, for edifying hours of feeding in front of Old Masters.

● **Churches:** can be quiet sanctuaries for nursing and discreet diaper changing.

● **Thrift stores:** generally tolerant of toddlers' meddling fingers, and cheap when you have to bribe them out of the house with the promise of a toy.

Protecting your posture

Start to remedy the bad back and aching shoulders of early motherhood with these carrying techniques, soothing alternatives to the hold that most of us naturally adopt, with baby resting near the heart on the left shoulder, which can lead to stiffness and stooping.

Flying angel hold

This pacifies colicky babies. Hold your baby horizontally with her back against your abdomen, looking outward. Place one arm under and around her chest (thumb and index finger supporting her top shoulder), head resting on your forearm, if necessary. Take your other hand between her legs, palm comforting her abdomen.

Facing-down hold

Good for restless evenings. From the flying angel, roll your baby down to face the floor, still supporting with one arm and hand around her chest, other hand on her abdomen. Swing rhythmically from foot to foot to comfort her.

Looking outward

Once she can support her head, hang your baby's arms over one forearm and lower her to your center of gravity, back resting against your abdomen. Support beneath her buttocks, if necessary. Now work on your posture. Place your feet hip-width apart, aligning your knees over your ankles. Exhaling, tilt your pelvis forward and up, bringing your hips in line with your knees. Lift from hips to underarms, tucking your abdominal muscles back to support your lower back. Broaden your chest and align your shoulders with your hips. Lift up from the back of your neck as if pulled by a string at the crown of the head.

Eating on the move

Turn out any mother's purse and, inevitably, you find a mush of squashed rice cakes, raisins, and spilt juice. The secret of stress-free journeys with kids is a bag stuffed with finger foods that keep the brain occupied and energy levels high. This doesn't have to be candy; for many months you can fool them with healthy treats. This list is good for children ranging from about one year to school age. When eating out with older babies, look for fabric slings that slot over the back of a restaurant chair and tie the child in place, and which can be folded up to fit in a pocket.

Caution: *avoid nuts if you have a family history of allergy and wherever you might come in contact with nut-allergic children.*

- Small boxes of raisins.
- Dried apricots and prunes.
- Assortment of nuts: encourage kids to be squirrels and sort the brazil nuts from the cashew nuts from the hazelnuts.
- Pots of cooked garbanzo beans and pitted olives.
- Sunflower and pumpkin seeds; also good for counting games.
- Tiny bunches of grapes.
- Punnets of fresh berries, such as raspberries and strawberries in season.

- Baby bananas and satsumas.
- Rice cakes and corn cakes, spread with butter and jelly, or peanut butter.
- Carrot and celery cut into sticks; snow peas.
- Cherry tomatoes and button mushrooms.
- Tiny fruit cakes and raisin-filled fingers.
- Cubes of cheese.
- Hard-cooked eggs.
- Mineral water bottles with sports spouts (endless amusement).

Posttravel massage

Traveling babies get strapped into strollers, slings, and car seats. At your destination, increase mobility with some rough and tumble play to warm and relax the muscles, then follow this massage to stretch the limbs. It can be performed fully clothed.

1 Place your baby on a soft surface on his back. Smile and tell him what you're going to do. Take one hand in each of your hands. Open them out to the sides, in line with his shoulders. Don't force it if your baby resists.

2 Cross his arms over his chest. Repeat the opening and closing movements until he loosens up, stretching slightly at the open position for a few seconds and pressing gently as you hold the arms crossed for a few seconds (vary the cross each time).

3 Hold your baby's left hand in your left hand. Take the right ankle in your right hand. Slowly pull the limbs away from each other to create a diagonal stretch. Don't force the movement.

4 Bring his leg and arm together, so left hand meets right knee. Hold briefly, then pull away, holding in the stretched position. Repeat, then repeat on the opposite limbs. To finish, give a big cuddle.

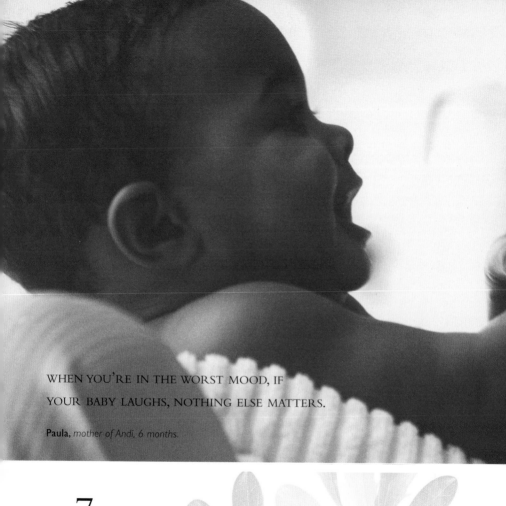

WHEN YOU'RE IN THE WORST MOOD, IF
YOUR BABY LAUGHS, NOTHING ELSE MATTERS.

Paula, *mother of Andi, 6 months.*

7

Playing

Learning through play

Early childhood is the time of life in which we learn most and most quickly because we are open to new experiences—75 percent of a child's brain development occurs between birth and two years. And the best way to learn is through play. This play isn't just beneficial for babies—it allows you to relive the carefree spontaneity you may last have experienced in your own childhood. You get to see the world afresh through the unjaundiced eyes of a child. Everything fascinates again: a bus journey, snowfall, a puddle on the sidewalk. On the walk to playgroup, instead of being disgruntled about living in a scruffy, down-at-heel neighborhood, we play the game "Wacky Wednesday" (after the Dr Seuss book), spotting strange things that shouldn't be on the sidewalk: tires and refrigerators, shoes and couches, a bag of fruit and a box of bagels. Even the less attractive side of life becomes something to laugh about with a child.

Baby yoga

Young babies love the whole-body stimulation and intense eye contact of baby yoga, specially adapted versions of hatha yoga postures that you ease your baby into. It makes them laugh, stimulates every body system, and wears them out: one class provides as much neuromuscular stimulation as a day's normal handling and carrying. Yoga babies show accelerated coordination, balance, and strength in the back and neck. Their concentration span and self-awareness increase, their curiosity is aroused, and their senses engaged. Many parents find the squeals of delight keep them coming back for more. From two months, use this taster to see if you want to search out a class.

1 Lie your baby on her back on a yoga mat, lambskin, or futon. Sit in front of her. Smile, explain what you are going to do, then give a soothing massage over her clothes (page 61).

2 Hold her lower legs and press her knees toward her chest. Hold briefly, repeat, then circle the legs left, then right.

3 Take one foot to the opposite hip or higher; don't force the movement. Repeat with the other leg.

4 Place her soles together, knees dropping outward, and take them toward her pelvis. Pull away and repeat. Then circle the legs to the left and right without moving the lower back.

5 With one foot in each hand, gently pull the legs toward you, then up. If she seems happy, lift the hips then let them flop to the floor. Repeat.

Toning exercises with baby

Don't expect to return to your prepregnancy size for months, even if other mothers seem to effortlessly. After the extreme effects of pregnancy—from tight-stretched belly to expanded heart and lungs—the body takes some restoring. And that's hard when you have no time, aren't sleeping, and a breastfeeding body demands extra calories. As your baby becomes more physically demanding, you'll shed pounds, but to kickstart toning, try these strengthening exercises from about two months after the birth. When you're stuck at home with a bored child, they recharge energy.

Baby sit-up

1 Lie on your back on the floor. Bend your knees, feet flat on the floor and hip-width apart. Prop your baby against your thighs, facing you. Keep your head and shoulders on the floor.

2 Exhaling, pull your abdominal muscles toward your lower back and lift your head and shoulders, rising slightly to look at your baby. Say "Hello."

3 Exhaling, lower to the floor. Repeat for as long as you can continue to pull back the abs or until your baby gets bored.

Flying baby

1 When you feel confident, from the same starting position lift your feet, lower legs together. Place your baby on your shins, stomach against your legs. Hold his hands.

2 Exhaling and pulling back your abdominal muscles, lift your head to look at your baby. Extend his arms and pull your knees toward you, singing out "Whee" as he flies.

3 Inhale as you take your legs back. Repeat until you are tired or he is bored.

Yoga for toddlers

When spirits are flagging and I can't think what to do with my kids, we practice yoga (of sorts). Even the one-year-old gets into it. We make bridges and crawl under them, or pretend to be dogs and cats. I feel reinvigorated afterward; they can't stop giggling. Try this easy routine.

1 Curl up on the floor like seeds. Gradually uncurl and grow into trees, arms extended, balancing on tiptoes.

2 Flop forward from the hips like scarecrows, head and shoulders relaxed, arms hanging loose.

3 Bend your knees, place palms on the floor, and do a few bunny hops.

4 Sit tall and stretch your legs wide. Lengthen your arms to the ceiling.

5 Bend your knees to bring your soles together. Grasp your toes with both hands and draw your knees toward your groin. Sit tall, flapping your knees up and down like butterflies.

6 Kneel on all fours. Lift your buttocks high, push back on your hands to stretch out of the shoulders, then relax your heels toward the floor like dogs. Making a howling noise.

7 Relax buttocks onto heels, arms stretched forward, then slink onto your front. Place palms beneath shoulders, then push forward and up to straighten the arms and raise your chest. Look to the ceiling and drop your hips like cobras, hissing "Ssss."

8 Sink your buttocks back on your heels, head down, hands resting by your feet. Place your hands on each other's lower back to feel the breath moving in and out.

Good play

Be free when you play, letting children set the agenda. A bossy, perfectionist parent stifles a child's creativity and confidence.

● **Chaos is healthy:** demanding that your child puts back one toy before she plays with another stifles the cross-creativity that urges children to mold plastiscine food for plastic horses, construct Lego towns in a sandpit, and shape shampoo-hairdos for soft toys in the bath. I recently heard of a mother driven to distraction by a thirteen-month-old who wouldn't tidy away his toys. That way madness lies.

● **Don't help too much:** when drawing together, let your child put eyes and mouth where she wants, and don't be tempted to finish that jigsaw. Be responsive but patient so she feels the success that comes with solving a problem by herself. To understand how deflating it is to have someone complete and perfect everything, play Lego with another adult and ask them to be bossy, telling you what to do, how to do it, and when. See how long it takes for you to get sulky and give up.

● **Spend time in your child's play space:** do just what she wants, no matter how crazy, for an hour each week. If she can run things in one room of the home, she may bow to rules elsewhere more readily.

● **Enjoy tidy-up time:** a lovely cry. Make a race of it, or a game, trying to match like with like and find its home.

Ways to amuse young children

Make a list of things your child loves doing, so you have plenty of ideas to hand when your brain and enthusiasm give up. Here are some things my kids enjoy.

For older babies:
- Reading a book.
- Peekaboo, Pat-a-Cake, tickling, and singing games.
- Toothbrush and a cup of water.
- Bowl of soapy water, sponge, and lots of plastic animals.
- Stacking boxes.
- Bag of odd things to sort: feathers and twigs, pine cones and corks, spoons and forks, cotton reels and popsicle sticks, pots of different sizes.
- Finger puppets.
- Music for dancing: mine love ska and Indian classical music.
- Chalk and a chalkboard.

For preschoolers:
- Colored paper, glue, stickers, and pens.
- Glittery fabric, feathers, ribbons, and sequins, for making hats and costumes.
- Lined writing paper and a "real" pen.
- Face painting.
- Wooden spoon puppets (draw a face and tie on fabric for clothes).
- Hide and Go Seek.
- Bouncing on the bed.
- Make gingerbread and decorate with frosting and silver balls, sugar sprinkles, candied cherries, chocolate drops, or a simple shaking of confectioners' sugar.
- Impromptu tents (draped sheets).
- Sing along to *The Sound of Music*.
- Dance to contrasting styles of classical music. The obvious ones work well: pieces such as Schubert's *The Trout*, Tchaikovsky's *The Nutcracker*, Saint-Saëns', *Carnival of the Animals*.

Get out of the house

No matter how stimulating your home, children feel stifled if they don't get out each day. Join a regular parent and toddler group, even if you usually hate organized activities, to give your child a chance to explore how other children and parents work, and to discover a new range of toys, especially big items such as climbing frames and messy water and sand trays. Children also get to test out (before the pressure of school) what it's like to share, wait for things, and sit still. In these kinds of relaxed but stimulating environments, which involve parents in play, children's social and communication skills flourish. You get to make friends, too, often with people in the local neighborhood whom you might never meet otherwise. Where else could you find yourself celebrating Eid with Muslim moms by sipping Caribbean fruit punch, and playing games organized by devout Catholics? Having young children is a great social entrée.

I made friends for the first time. Playgroup is not just for children, it's for us mothers.

Hayley, *mother of Tarik, 6, Hannah and Laura, 4.*

ONCE I MET ANOTHER MOM WITH TWINS AND WE FOUND A MUSIC CLASS TO GET OUT TO, I FELT MORE ABLE TO COPE.

Pina, *mother of Emilia and Olivia, 2.*

The first birthday

This is as much about marking a year as parent as fêting the new one-year-old (although they love it when you sing to them). Invite adult friends for a celebration after the relative seclusion of the first year. Children's parties thereafter involve jello, party bags, and screaming, so enjoy the relative normality.

● **Serve your favorite tipple:** and a decadent adult cake.

● **Hold a ceremony at the time of the birth:** invite those who were there. We placed our first daughter on the spot where she was born on the kitchen floor, lit a candle, and sang.

● **Write a letter to your one-year–old:** describe his face, first words, and friends.

● **Remember significant days:** perfect summer outings, night dashes to the ER, first smiles and teeth.

● **Record your feelings:** how has it been to be a mother all year? Mourn the loss of your newborn, then rejoice in the wonder of the one-year-old.

● **Replay your mental film of the birth:** don't be ashamed to shed tears, and feel the fear.

● **Perform a cleansing ritual:** prune your baby's wardrobe of outgrown garments. Make piles for heirlooms, to give away, and to keep for special memories (that stain!). Put one pile aside for quilting when you have time.

● **Give a personal gift:** not another hunk of plastic, but a shell from a favorite beach, a leaf you found together, a pebble with his initial on. Save in a special box as talismans for life.

I GOT TO A YEAR AND FINALLY
RELAXED; SURELY NOTHING CAN TOP
WHAT WE WENT THROUGH IN THOSE
FIRST 12 MONTHS?

Monica, *mother of Paco, 13 months.*

8

Relaxing and refinding yourself

"Me" time

Both full-time motherhood and juggling work with children can make for "grumpy mom." The whole family benefits when a mother is relaxed, so you owe it to your loved ones to take some "me" time, for a yoga class, girl's night out, or couch-potato session. Motherhood offers few opportunities simply to do nothing. Hour upon hour, we're subject to sensory overload: someone is always talking, shouting or crying, smelling bad, demanding a cuddle or to be carried, needing to be kept an eye on. And we live in anticipation of the future: washing up after breakfast means thinking about what to make for lunch. The constant repetition of the same demands—washing, cooking, clearing up, brushing hair—turns even the most placid, good-natured person into a nagging harridan who can only bark orders. I sometimes forget to exhale with the constant activity and anticipation. To stay sane and happy, we all need a little silence and solitude, and to spend time in the present focusing on nothing but the task in hand. Then you finally have chance to breathe out.

Relaxed breathing

When your baby is asleep on you, try a relaxation technique that brings you in tune with your baby's breathing pattern. This calming exercise is particularly good for dads who feel left out of the mother-baby love fest. The nonverbal communication it promotes not only reduces stress and anxiety, but increases confidence in your intuitive ability to care for and love your child.

1 When your baby is asleep, close your eyes and start to tune in to her breathing pattern, allowing it to erase other thoughts from your mind.

2 After listening for a while and feeling the breath expanding your baby's abdomen and back, start to link breaths. Inhale for two or three of your baby's breaths; exhale for two or three. Don't hold your breath, and let the in-breath come naturally, without grabbing at it. Feel the inhalation expand your lower abdomen, and feel your abdominal muscles drawing back toward your spine as you breathe out.

3 Notice how your in- and out-breaths lengthen and slow as you become more relaxed. Start to extend the out-breath, breathing in for two or three of your baby's breaths, and breathing out for three or four.

4 Continue for 3–5 minutes, or until you fall asleep, too.

Switching off

At least once a week, you need an hour to forget about everything except yourself. Whether you head to the gym, open a bottle of wine, have a haircut, or hit the shoestore is of no matter: just do something you crave that nourishes you alone and allows you to be selfish for a while. If it gets you out of the house, so much the better. This can take some planning. Write it into your diary well ahead, booking someone to cover the childcare. Arrange childcare swaps with a friend—it's often less complicated to look after two children of the same age than one. And don't forfeit this time for anything other than the most urgent emergency.

Sounds of stillness

When you crave space and silence but can't get away from the madness of everyday life with young children, repeat the mantra of peace "*Om shanti, shanti, shanti*" under your breath. This is thought to alleviate mental and nervous stress and anxiety, and to rebalance mind, body, and spirit by nurturing calmness, detachment, and contentment.

Doing nothing

The best of times sometimes happen when you don't plan any activities. You lounge in front of daytime TV reading a trashy magazine; the children throw cushions around, jump on the couch, and decorate Barbie with nail polish. Don't hothouse kids all the time, tempting though this is, particularly with an only child. Children left to their own devices become more self-starting, inventive, and imaginative, and less reliant on adults to steer every activity.

Mother and baby retreat

French mothers may spend some time on retreat at a convent when their babies are young. The nuns care for the babies between feeds, while the mothers do nothing but nurture themselves, reading and sleeping, walking in the countryside, and eating good food. If you can't take a trip to France, try this home retreat.

1 Arrange for a trusted person—your mother, best friend, a godparent, or an aunt perhaps—to come to stay for the weekend. She has to be willing to be up at all hours doing the bulk of the childcare, and will need an assistant (your partner, her husband?) to look after her.

2 After feeding your child on the first morning, pass him over and spend the day doing exactly what you want: a bath or swim, gardening or reading, dozing whenever you wish. Order in takeaways so no one has to cook or wash dishes.

3 Go to bed early, safe in the knowledge that someone will bring you the baby if he needs to breastfeed. Give up the responsibility gladly, and make sure you get a lie-in and breakfast in bed.

4 Repeat on the second day, if everyone agrees, spending time on pampering beauty treatments: get a pedicure, have your legs waxed, enjoy a facial or massage so you look as relaxed as you feel.

5 Shower thank-you gifts on your carers, and take back your child. Repeat yearly.

Walking meditation

Sometimes the only time I get in the day when no one is bombarding me with questions is when I'm walking with a child in the stroller. Here, for a moment, it's possible to find tranquility in the midst of action, with each step sensing a purposeful autonomy and the freedom of the space above and around you.

1 As you walk, switch off from other demands. Stop anticipating what comes next or mulling over what you've just done. Watch how your breath flows in and out, and notice how it coordinates naturally with your footsteps.

2 Move outside yourself, becoming aware of the natural world—the sky and clouds, the temperature, the season. When thoughts occur, imagine them as clouds passing across a blue sky and let them float on.

3 Become aware of your pace: your feet lifting and touching the ground. Feel the different parts of your foot against the

floor. Sense the suppleness of your body and your innate sense of balance as your weight passes from one side of the body to the other.

4 Now focus on your breathing, inhaling easily for two paces and exhaling smoothly for two paces. Feel your thoughts become steady with your constant pace. Quiet your mind and heart until you find yourself doing nothing but moving in meditation.

Refinding yourself

When my first child was eighteen months old, I realized that when I thought about her, I visualized a 60ft giant, so in awe of her were we. Although our children rightly take center stage in our lives, it's not healthy for them to rule our world. The time comes to take stock and think about our role as adults and parents. It's hard to find time to step back and reassess—with young children, the all-encompassing day-to-day minutiae so completely absorb us in every stage of babyhood that we can't remember how life was two weeks ago, let alone foresee how things will change in another two months. Yet it's vital to retain a sense of the person you were before you became a mother, and to ponder the changing priorities that make you who you are now.

I hankered after my old self, who wore grown-up shoes and didn't have vomit down her left shoulder. Then I met some work friends for a drink. After an hour, it dawned on me that the office life was the boring one. I was out of the loop, and the gossip about who did what paled into insignificance compared with how my life had changed and how I felt about my baby.

Jo, *mother of Martha, 10 months.*

Going back to work

Most mothers feel ambiguous about this. Part of us is desperate to return to the adult world, with its peace, space to focus and achieve, and time to drink coffee and gossip by the water cooler. At the same time, we can't imagine leaving a baby. Working while you have young children is difficult, and "having it all" is almost impossible. Even if you can afford daycare, you may not feel happy leaving a child for many hours. Many women find more flexible employment during this lifestage. Working part-time, freelance, in a job-share, or from home, keeps you within the labor market, but in a more piecemeal way so you can be more family oriented. Keep your vision of the possibilities flexible, trading time for money for a while. The bonus of motherhood is super-efficiency—there's nothing like caring for a baby to teach you how to shoehorn immense amounts into two minutes—and office politics never seem as all-consuming. Having a perspective on what's really important in life makes you more incisive and demanding, and brings the confidence to take calculated risks and cut the crap. If less remunerative, this new work–life balance is at least more realistic.

I'M STILL COMING TO TERMS WITH NOT BEING ABLE TO COMMIT TO A NINE TO FIVE JOB. I JUST DON'T WANT MY DAUGHTER TO BE SHUNTED BETWEEN MINDERS BEFORE AND AFTER SCHOOL EVERY DAY.

Mary, *mother of Iris, 7.*

Having another baby

I spent my second pregnancy racked with guilt about destroying my first daughter's security, ruining her life by introducing a usurper into the home. The feeling grew with my belly, becoming almost unbearable toward the end of the pregnancy. The relief when I delivered this tiny thing that looked nothing like her sister and just lay sleeping, completely undemanding, flooded the house. Despite the logistics, two children seemed easier to cope with than one. As the telescopic focus of energy, hope, and anxiety on the first child expanded, she was given space to breathe and develop by herself at last, and became more resourceful and less shy. And she gained a best friend as her younger sister grew older. With a second child you have the benefit of experience. You know to leave a sleeping newborn be rather than worry she'll never wake. Whereas, with the first baby, you looked ahead, longing for each new stage, now you appreciate how fleeting and wonderful the first short weeks are, and savor the hours, knowing that if you blink, you miss an entire developmental stage. Above all, you worry less, especially about not having enough love to go round: each new birth seems to open up a fresh and neverending store of love.

How come we all feel so overwhelmed with the first baby? All they do is eat and sleep.

Christie, *mother of Sol, 2, and Abe, 2 months.*

Rediscovering your relationship

Pregnancy can be an intensely "coupley" period in which you share everything: hopes and anxieties, pride and anticipation, carefree sex and lazy lie-ins. Birth changes everything. You find yourself stuck in bed while he's out celebrating with your friends. You no longer share every task, and your spheres are not mutual and equal. He usually remains in the outside world of work, friends, wages, and release from domesticity. For a while, you wallow in the home, reverting to a prehistoric gender role. Confusion, resentment, and misunderstandings can grow, and romance may become just another chore at the end of another exhausting day. Some time soon, set aside an evening to spend as a couple. Get the baby to bed early and unplug the TV. Oust older kids from your bed so you can have a cuddle. Reserve one night a week for a takeaway and movie. Ask grandparents to cover bedtime so you can sit in a bar from lunchtime to closing time. Go dancing if that's what fired you up before children. Or grab a naughty moment while children are playing in another room—being parents of young children can make you feel like teenagers again. And that's exciting. As your energy and enthusiasm return, and with practice, you may even find subjects to talk about beside babies. All relationships change; rediscovering what you have now gives you a chance to start afresh.

Letting go

Children love good childminders. Instead of shouting, "Hang on a minute, I've just got to paint this windowframe/put in the washing/stir this pan," they get out paints and brushes, farm animals, or dressing-up clothes, and play with your child face to face. One local minder dresses her charges in Indian saris and ankle bells, and they dance to Bollywood movies. A child who normally won't touch anything but fries greedily tucks in to rice and peas at the home of his Jamaican "granny." Good childminders (those who don't park kids in front of the TV) teach children skills you'd never think of, and your child becomes part of a wider family, subsumed into the community in a way you'll never be. To ease the transition, tell a minder about your child's routines, special songs, naptimes, and foods, and ask that she weave them into the day. Start an activity, such as a painting, before you go to work, and finish it when you get home to give much-needed continuity. Don't hover about, trying to decide when is a good moment to go, but have confidence in the leaving; if you don't feel positive, how will your child? Hide outside the door, if necessary, for five minutes, and listen to any screams subsiding. Return to pick up your child just before you're supposed to and you can eavesdrop on his contented chatting in his new domain.

IT IS THE HEART THAT GIVES, THE FINGERS JUST LET GO.

Nigerian proverb

Finding a new you

Today, many of us don't feel grown up when we leave home, get a job, or marry. When you become a mother and finally accept the adult responsibility of putting yourself on hold for a while, it can be oddly liberating. After spending twenty years obsessing about your life, career, and relationships, it's a relief to lose yourself in play, in a child's smiles, in the moment. And as your infant gradually develops her own character, so motherhood gives you months to rethink who you are. To reassess your own childhood and the characteristics that arose from its influences. To develop qualities more appropriate to life now, and jettison unhelpful ways of behaving and thinking.

Assessing who you are now

1 Look back on the time since the birth. How have you changed? List the qualities you've discovered, good and bad. Write down the valuable qualities you would like to develop and give reasons why.

2 On a separate sheet of paper, write down the characteristics you would like to let go. Burn the paper; as it turns to ashes, vow to move on to a new, more positive approach to life.

When Louis was tiny, a woman said, "When they reach six months you get yourself back." Nonsense, I thought, I'm still me. But after the six-month mark, when I was working part-time and nursing less, her words came back. I had lost some "me-ness" without knowing it. And it wasn't a bad thing.

Val, *mother of Louis, 9 months.*

Resources

Good reading

A LIFE'S WORK: ON BECOMING A MOTHER Rachel Cusk, 2002, London, Fourth Estate

LIFE AFTER BIRTH: WHAT EVEN YOUR FRIENDS WON'T TELL YOU ABOUT MOTHERHOOD Kate Figes, 1998, London, Penguin

PARANOID PARENTING: ABANDON YOUR ANXIETIES AND BE A GOOD PARENT Frank Furedi, 2001, London, Penguin

THE BLUE JAY'S DANCE: A BIRTH YEAR Louise Erdrich, 1995, New York, HarperCollins

Invaluable manuals

BABY MASSAGE: THE CALMING POWER OF TOUCH Dr. Alan Heath and Nicki Bainbridge, 2000, London, Dorling Kindersley

BABY YOGA: GENTLE EXERCISE FOR BABIES, MUMS AND DADS Françoise Barbira Freedman, 2000, London, Gaia Books

SOLVE YOUR CHILD'S SLEEP PROBLEMS Dr. Richard Ferber, 1986, New York, Fireside

Reassuring internet sites

www.badmothers-club.co.uk
"Retell therapy" for moments when you need confirmation that "It's not just me."
www.babycenter.com
Advice on every aspect of parenting from experts and other mothers.

Picture credits

Page 2 © Robert Llewellyn/CORBIS; Page 7 © Ronnie Kaufman/CORBIS; Pages 8–9 © Strauss/Curtis/CORBIS; Page 19 © Tim Pannell/CORBIS; Pages 24–25 © Jose Luis Pelaez, Inc./CORBIS; Pages 34–35 © Curtis Graham/CORBIS; Pages 44–45 © Steve Prezant/CORBIS; Pages 54–55 © Stephen Parker; Pages 64–65 © LWA-Dann Tardif/CORBIS; Pages 72–73 © Ariel Skelley/CORBIS; Pages 82–83 © Don Mason/CORBIS; Page 95 © Barbara Peacock/CORBIS